Me & My Sister

Fun quilts

Quilting is always a pleasant pastime, but making these quilts from Me and My Sister Designs is just plain fun! Who wouldn't love to create a candy-colored quilt from simple four-patch and triangle-square blocks? And who wouldn't enjoy owning a quilt covered in yellow rubber duckies? From the sweetly feminine Buttermints to the whimsically colorful Orange Slices, you'll find a quilt in this collection that's perfect for everyone you know.

LEISURE ARTS, INC.
Little Rock, Arkansas

Table of Contents

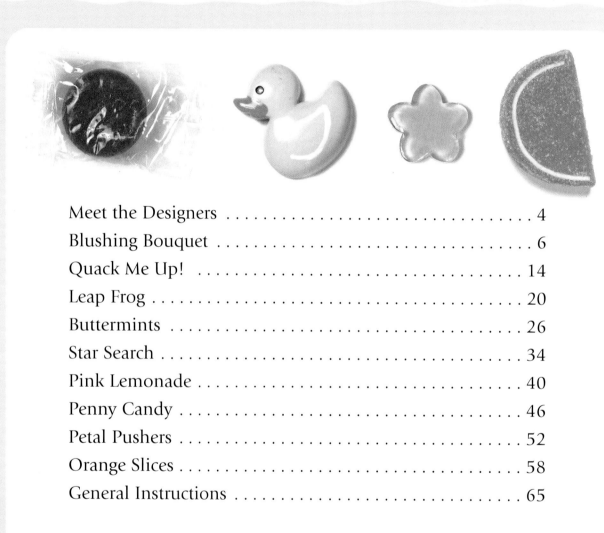

4

6

14

20

26

34

40

46

52

58

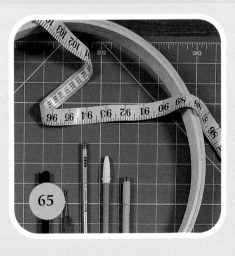

65

4

Meet the Designers

Have you ever dreamed of having a job that allowed you to work in your pajamas?

Barbara Groves and Mary Jacobson, the owners of *Me and My Sister Designs,* have realized that dream. For the sisters, it seems like a bit of serendipity that started with their interest in quilting. However, full-time quilt designing is a goal they only realized after years of hard work.

"Even when we lived far apart, our love of fabrics, sewing, and quilting remained a bond we shared," says Mary. "When a move back to Phoenix brought the two of us together again, we started thinking that there is nothing like owning a quilt shop to increase your fabric stash. So we opened a store."

To promote the new fabrics they stocked at their store, the sisters began designing quilt patterns as give-aways. Their quilt shop was a success, and Barbara and Mary enjoyed the work.

"But running a quilt shop is an all-or-nothing venture," says Barbara. "It had to have our entire focus to remain successful. After four years, we knew it was time to close the shop and do something a little less demanding, like designing quilts from our homes.

"That's when we decided to put our promotional patterns into a book. To help us, Mary's husband put each quilt pattern on its own CD-ROM. That really got us thinking — why not sell the patterns this way?

"We took our first patterns on CD to the 2003 Quilt Market in Houston. Within hours, we were picked up by all the major distributors." Barbara says. "And now, nine of our quilts are in this Leisure Arts book. It's so exciting to see our patterns become available in both kinds of media. We're also designing fabrics for Moda. Our first fabric line is named *Petal Pushers*. We'll soon have a total of four lines of fabrics. We've come full circle, and it's fabulous."

Visit Barbara and Mary's Website at www.meandmysisterdesigns.com to learn about their newest fabric lines from Moda Fabric.

Barbara Groves and Mary Jacobson

Blushing
Bouquet

Finished Quilt Size: 95" x 95" (241 cm x 241 cm)
Finished Block Size: 14¹/₄" x 14¹/₄" (36 cm x 36 cm)

Yardage Requirements

Yardage is based on 43"/44" (109 cm/112 cm) wide fabric with a "usable" width of 40" (102 cm) after trimming selvages and shrinkage.

7¹/₂ yds (6.9 m) **total** of assorted print fabrics
4¹/₂ yds (4.1 m) pink print fabric
8⁵/₈ yds (7.9 m) of fabric for backing

You will also need:

103" x 103" (262 cm x 262 cm) square of batting

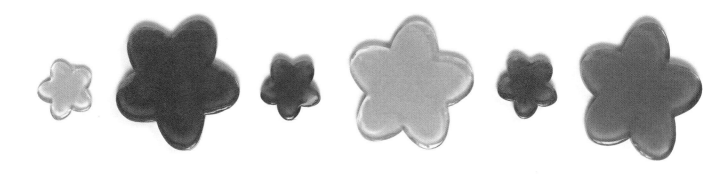

Blushing Bouquet

CUTTING OUT THE PIECES

*Follow **Rotary Cutting**, page 66, to cut fabric. All measurements include $^1/_4$" seam allowances.*

From assorted print fabrics:
- Cut 32 **large rectangles** $8^3/_4$" x $4^3/_8$".
- Cut 50 squares 8" x 8". Cut each square **once** diagonally to make 100 **small triangles**.
- Cut 200 **small squares** $2^7/_8$" x $2^7/_8$".
- Cut 8 **medium rectangles** $2^1/_8$" x 8".
- Cut 192 **small rectangles** 2" x 8".

From pink print fabric:
- Cut 5 strips $6^1/_2$" wide. From these strips, cut 25 **large squares** $6^1/_2$" x $6^1/_2$".
- Cut 16 strips $2^7/_8$" wide. From these strips, cut 200 **small squares** $2^7/_8$" x $2^7/_8$".
- Cut 18 **border strips** $2^1/_2$" wide.
- Cut 10 **binding strips** $2^1/_4$" wide.

ASSEMBLING THE BLOCKS

*Follow **Piecing**, page 67, and **Pressing**, page 68. Measurements given throughout assembly include outer seam allowances. Use a $^1/_4$" seam allowance throughout.*

Block A

1. Draw a diagonal line (corner to corner) on wrong side of each pink print **small square**. With right sides together, place a pink print **small square** on top of an assorted print **small square**. Stitch seam $^1/_4$" from each side of drawn line (**Fig. 1**).

Fig. 1

2. Cut along drawn line and press open to make 2 **Triangle-Squares**. Make 400 **Triangle-Squares**. Triangle-Squares should measure $2^1/_2$" x $2^1/_2$".

Triangle-Squares (make 400)

3. Sew 3 assorted **Triangle-Squares** together to make **Unit 1**. Make 100 **Unit 1's**. Unit 1's should measure $6^1/_2$" x $2^1/_2$".

Unit 1 (make 100)

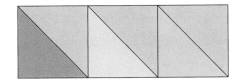

4. Sew 1 **Unit 1** and 2 assorted **Triangle-Squares** together to make **Unit 2**. Make 50 **Unit 2's**. Unit 2's should measure $10^1/_2$" x $2^1/_2$".

Unit 2 (make 50)

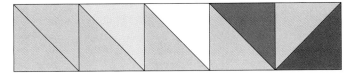

5. Sew 1 **Unit 1** on each side of 1 pink print **large square** to make **Unit 3**. Make 25 **Unit 3's**. Unit 3's should measure $10^1/_2$" x $6^1/_2$".

Unit 3 (make 25)

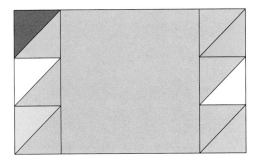

6. Sew 2 **Unit 2's** and 1 **Unit 3** together to make **Unit 4**. Make 25 **Unit 4's**. Unit 4's should measure $10^1/_2$" x $10^1/_2$".

Unit 4 (make 25)

7. Sew one **small triangle** to each side of a
    Unit 4 to make **Block A**. Make 25 **Block A's**.
    Block A's should measure 14³/₄" x 14³/₄".

Block A (make 25)

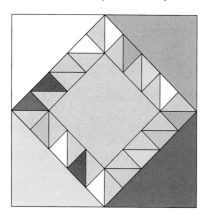

Corner Block

1. Sew 5 **small rectangles** together to make
    Unit 5. Make 8 **Unit 5's**. Unit 5's should
    measure 8" x 8".

Unit 5 (make 8)

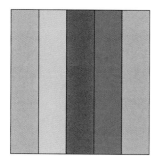

2. Draw a diagonal line (corner to corner) on
    wrong side of 4 **Unit 5's**. With right sides
    together and seamlines aligned, place a
    marked **Unit 5** on top of an unmarked **Unit 5**
    (**Fig. 2**). Stitch along drawn line.

Fig. 2

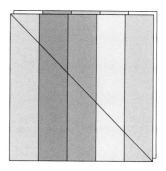

3. Trim ¹/₄" from one side of drawn line (**Fig. 3**)
    and press open to make **Corner Block**. Make
    4 **Corner Blocks**. Corner Blocks should
    measure 8" x 8".

Fig. 3

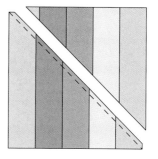

Corner Block (make 4)

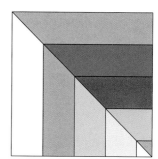

Hourglass Block

. Referring to **Triangle Cutting Diagram**, mark center of 1 long (top) edge of 1 **large rectangle**. Cut from bottom corners to top center to make **large triangle**. Make 32 large triangles.

Triangle Cutting Diagram

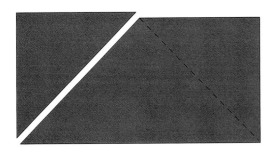

. Sew 4 **large triangles** together to make **Hourglass Blocks**. Make 8 **Hourglass Blocks**. Hourglass Blocks should measure 8" x 8".

Hourglass Block (make 8)

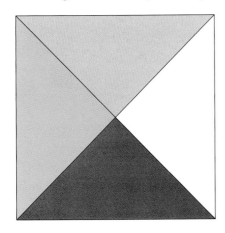

ASSEMBLING THE QUILT TOP CENTER

*Refer to **Quilt Top Diagram**, page 13, for placement.*

1. Sew 5 **Block A's** together to make a **Row**. Make 5 **Rows**. Row should measure $71^3/_4$" x $14^3/_4$".
2. Sew **Rows** together to make **Quilt Top Center**. Quilt Top Center should measure $71^3/_4$" x $71^3/_4$".

ADDING THE BORDERS
Inner Borders

1. Using diagonal seams (**Fig. 4**), sew 8 **border strips** together end to end to make 1 continuous **inner border strip**.

Fig. 4

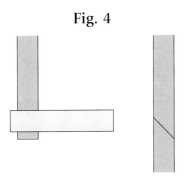

2. To determine length of **inner side borders**, measure *length* across center of quilt top center. From continuous inner border strip, cut 2 **inner side borders** the determined length. Matching centers and corners, sew **inner side borders** to quilt top center.
3. To determine length of **inner top/bottom borders**, measure *width* across center of quilt top center (including added borders). From continuous inner border strip, cut 2 **inner top/bottom borders** the determined length. Matching centers and corners, sew **inner top/bottom borders** to quilt top center.

Middle Borders

1. Sew 10 **small rectangles** and 1 **medium rectangle** together to make **Unit 7**. Make 8 **Unit 7's**. Unit 7 should measure $17^1/8$" x 8".

Unit 7 (make 8)

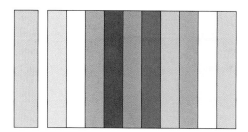

2. Sew 18 **small rectangles** together to make **Unit 8**. Make 4 **Unit 8's**. Unit 8 should measure $27^1/2$" x 8".

Unit 8 (make 4)

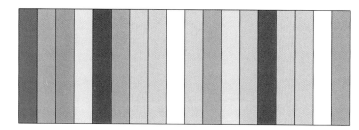

3. Sew 2 **Unit 7's**, 2 **Hourglass Blocks**, and 1 **Unit 8** together to make **Middle Border**. Make 4 **Middle Borders**. Middle border should measure $75^3/4$" x 8".

4. Matching centers and corners, sew 1 **middle border** to each side of Quilt Top Center. Make adjustments to border length by making a few seams smaller or larger if needed.

5. Sew 1 **Corner Block** to each end of 1 **middle border**. Repeat for remaining middle border.

6. Matching centers and corners, sew remaining **borders** to top and bottom of Quilt Top Center. Make adjustments to border length by making a few seams smaller or larger if needed.

Outer Borders

1. Using remaining 10 **border strips**, repeat **Inner Borders**, page 11, Steps 1 – 3, to attach outer borders.

COMPLETING THE QUILT

1. Follow **Quilting**, page 68, to mark, layer, and quilt as desired. Our quilt is machine quilted with meandering leaves and flowers.

2. Follow **Binding**, page 73, to bind quilt using **binding strips**.

Middle Border (make 4)

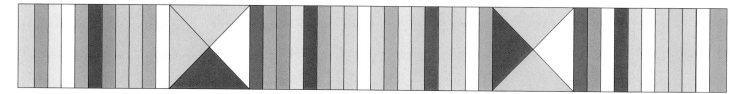

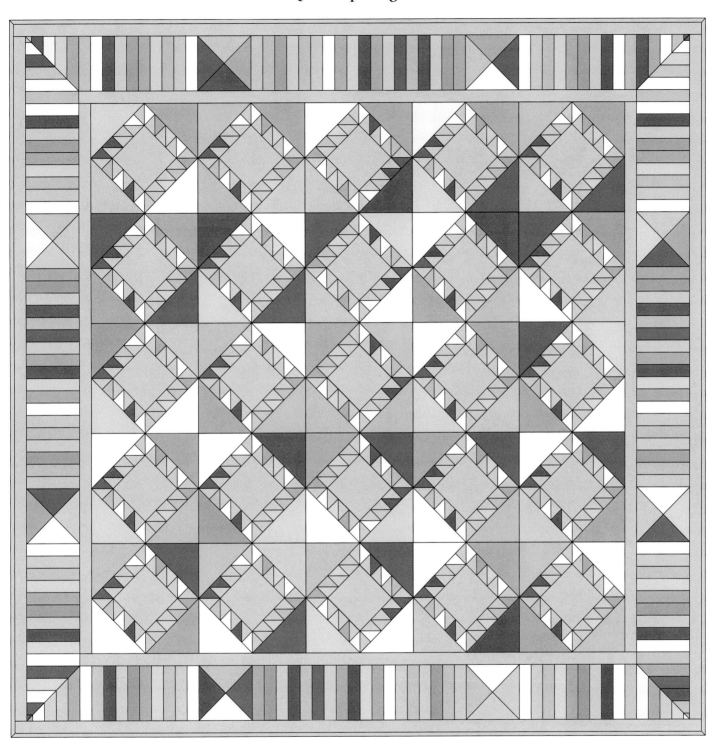

Quack Me Up!

Finished Quilt Size: 70½" x 78½" (179 cm x 199 cm)

Yardage Requirements

Yardage is based on 43"/44" (109 cm/112 cm) wide fabric with a "usable" width of 40" (102 cm) after trimming selvages and shrinkage.

1¼ yds (1.1 m) yellow print fabric for pinwheels

1¼ yds (1.1 m) white print fabric for pinwheels

1⅝ yds (1.5 m) **total** of assorted blue and yellow print fabrics for bars

2¾ yds (2.5 m) novelty print fabric

4⅞ yds (4.5 m) of fabric for backing

⅝ yd (57 cm) of fabric for binding

You will also need:

79" x 87" (201 cm x 221 cm) rectangle of batting

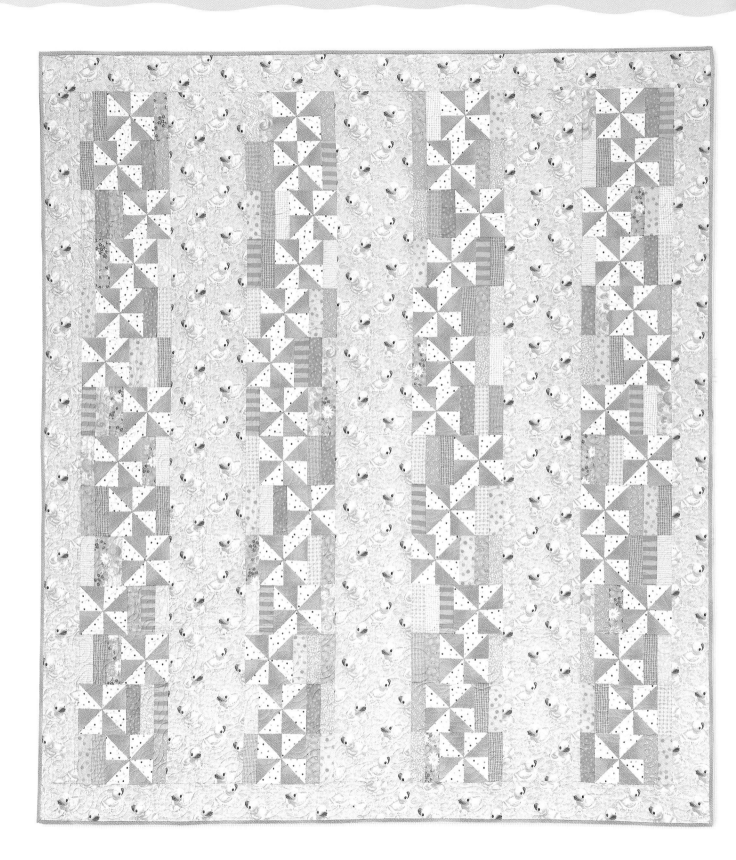

Me Up!

CUTTING OUT THE PIECES

Follow **Rotary Cutting**, page 66, to cut fabric. All measurements include $^1/_4$" seam allowances.

From yellow print fabric:
- Cut 11 strips $3^3/_8$" wide. From these strips, cut 112 **squares** $3^3/_8$" x $3^3/_8$".

From white print fabric:
- Cut 11 strips $3^3/_8$" wide. From these strips, cut 112 **squares** $3^3/_8$" x $3^3/_8$".

From assorted blue and yellow print fabrics:
- Cut 168 **bars** 2" x $5^1/_2$".

From novelty print fabric:
- Cut 4 *crosswise* **top/bottom border strips** $4^1/_4$" x 40".
- Cut 3 *lengthwise* **sashings** $8^1/_2$" x $70^1/_2$".
- Cut 2 *lengthwise* **side borders** $4^1/_4$" x $70^1/_2$".

From fabric for binding:
- Cut 8 **binding strips** $2^1/_4$" wide.

ASSEMBLING THE BLOCKS

*Follow **Piecing**, page 67, and **Pressing**, page 68. Measurements given throughout assembly include outer seam allowances. Use a $^1/_4$" seam allowance throughout.*

1. Draw a diagonal line (corner to corner) on wrong side of each white **square**. With right sides together, place a white **square** on top of a yellow **square**. Stitch seam $^1/_4$" from each side of drawn line (**Fig. 1**).

Fig. 1

2. Cut along drawn line and press open to make 2 **Triangle-Squares**. Triangle-Square should measure 3" x 3". Make 224 **Triangle-Squares**.

Triangle-Squares (make 224)

3. Sew 4 **Triangle-Squares** together to make a **Pinwheel**. Pinwheels should measure $5^1/2$" x $5^1/2$". Make 56 **Pinwheels**.

Pinwheel (make 56)

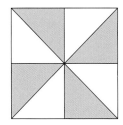

4. Sew 3 **bars** and 1 **Pinwheel** together to make **Unit 1**. Unit 1 should measure $5^1/2$" x 10". Make 24 **Unit 1's**.

Unit 1 (make 24)

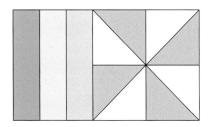

5. Sew 3 **bars** and 1 **Pinwheel** together to make **Unit 2**. Unit 2 should measure $5^1/2$" x 10". Make 32 **Unit 2's**.

Unit 2 (make 32)

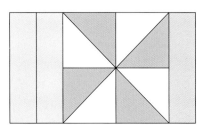

ASSEMBLING THE QUILT TOP CENTER

*Refer to **Quilt Top Diagram** for placement.*

1. Positioning Units as desired, sew a total of 14 **Unit 1's** and **Unit 2's** together to make a vertical **Row**. Make 4 **Rows**. Rows should measure $70^1/2$" long. Make adjustments to Row length by making a few seams between Units slightly smaller or larger if needed.
2. Sew 4 **Rows** and 3 **Sashings** together to make **Quilt Top Center**. Quilt Top Center should measure $62^1/2$" x $70^1/2$".

ADDING THE BORDERS

1. Matching centers and corners, sew **side borders** to quilt top center.
2. Using diagonal seams (**Fig. 2**), sew top/bottom border strips together end to end to make 1 continuous **border strip**. From continuous border strip, cut 2 **top/bottom borders** 70" long. Matching centers and corners, sew **top/bottom borders** to quilt top center.

Fig. 2

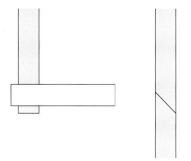

COMPLETING THE QUILT

1. Follow **Quilting**, page 68, to mark, layer, and quilt as desired. Our quilt is machine quilted with a meandering swirl pattern.
2. Follow **Binding**, page 73, to bind quilt using **binding strips**.

Quilt Top Diagram

Leap Frog

Finished Quilt Size: 81" x 87" (206 cm x 221 cm)
Finished Block Size: 8" x 10" (20 cm x 25 cm)

Yardage Requirements

Yardage is based on 43"/44" (109 cm/112 cm) wide fabric with a "usable" width of 40" (102 cm) after trimming selvages and shrinkage.

> 5 yds (4.6 m) **total** of assorted print fabrics
> 3³/₄ yds (3.4 m) of white solid fabric
> 7¹/₂ yds (6.9 m) fabric for backing

You will also need:

> 89" x 95" (226 cm x 241 cm) rectangle of batting

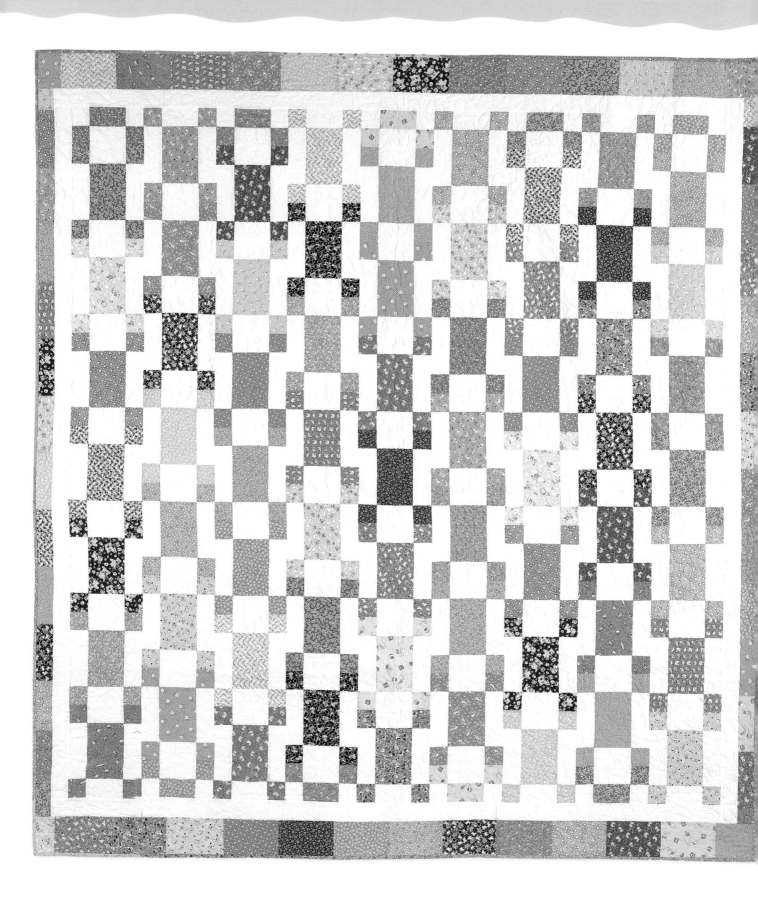

Frog

CUTTING OUT THE PIECES

*Follow **Rotary Cutting**, page 66, to cut fabric. All measurements include $^1/_4$" seam allowances.*

From assorted print fabrics:
- Cut 68 sets of 1 **rectangle** $4^1/_2$" x $6^1/_2$" and 4 **squares** $2^1/_2$" x $2^1/_2$". (Each set should be cut from 1 fabric.)
- Cut 28 **rectangles** $2^1/_2$" x $6^1/_2$".
- Cut 28 **rectangles** $4^1/_2$" x $6^1/_2$".
- For binding, cut $2^1/_4$"w **binding strips** of various lengths to equal 360" when sewn together end to end.

From white solid fabric:
- Cut 48 **strips** $2^1/_2$" wide. From 23 of these strips, cut 136 **rectangles** $2^1/_2$" x $6^1/_2$". From 17 of these strips, cut 136 **rectangles** $2^1/_2$" x $4^1/_2$". Leave 8 strips uncut for inner borders.

ASSEMBLING THE BLOCKS

*Follow **Piecing**, page 67, and **Pressing**, page 68. Use a $^1/_4$" seam allowance throughout. Measurements given throughout assembly include outer seam allowances. Use 1 set of matching fabric pieces to make each Block.*

1. Sew 2 **squares** and 1 white $2^1/_2$" x $4^1/_2$" **rectangle** together to make **Unit 1**. Make 2 **Unit 1's**. Unit 1 should measure $2^1/_2$" x $8^1/_2$".

Unit 1 (make 2)

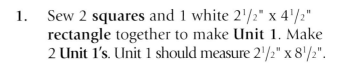

2. Sew 2 white $2^1/_2$" x $6^1/_2$" **rectangles** and 1 print $4^1/_2$" x $6^1/_2$" **rectangle** together to make **Unit 2**. Unit 2 should measure $8^1/_2$" x $6^1/_2$".

Unit 2

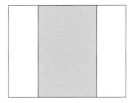

3. Sew 2 **Unit 1's** and **Unit 2** together to make **Block**. Block should measure $8^1/_2$" x $10^1/_2$".

Block

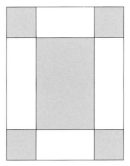

4. Repeat **Steps 1 – 3** to make 68 **Blocks**.
5. Trim 5 of these Blocks as shown in **Fig. 1** to make **Staggered Blocks**. Discard center segment. You will use 9 Staggered Blocks; discard 1. Staggered Blocks should measure 8$^1/_2$" x 4$^1/_2$".

Fig. 1

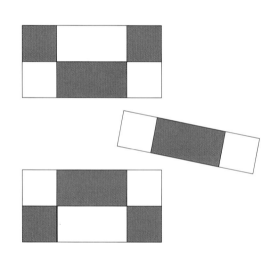

4 $^1/_2$ Inches

4 $^1/_2$ Inches

Staggered Block (make 9)

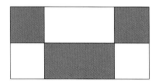 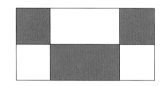

ASSEMBLING THE QUILT TOP CENTER

1. Sew 7 **Blocks** and 1 **Staggered Block** together to make a vertical **Row**. Make 9 **Rows**. Rows should measure 74$^1/_2$" long. Make adjustments to Row length if needed by making a few seams between Blocks slightly larger or smaller.

Row (make 9)

2. Turning each Row in the opposite direction, sew **Rows** together to make **Quilt Top Center**. Quilt Top Center should measure 72$^1/_2$" x 74$^1/_2$".

ADDING THE BORDERS
Inner Borders

1. Using diagonal seams (**Fig. 2**), sew 8 white 2$^1/_2$"w **strips** together end to end to make 1 continuous **inner border strip**.

Fig. 2

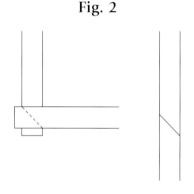

2. To determine length of **inner side borders**, measure *length* across center of quilt top center. From continuous inner border strip, cut 2 **inner side borders** the determined length. Matching centers and corners, sew **inner side borders** to quilt top center.
3. To determine length of **inner top/bottom borders**, measure *width* across center of quilt top center (including added borders). From continuous inner border strip, cut 2 **inner top/bottom borders** the determined length. Matching centers and corners, sew **inner top/bottom borders** to quilt top center.

Outer Borders

1. Matching short edges, sew 14 print rectangles 2¹/₂" x 6¹/₂" together to make **Outer Side Border**. Make 2 **Outer Side Borders**.

2. To determine length of **outer side borders**, measure *length* across center of quilt top center. Trim **outer side borders** the determined length. Matching centers and corners, sew **outer side borders** to quilt top center.

3. Matching short edges, sew 14 print rectangles 4¹/₂" x 6¹/₂" together to make **Outer Top/Bottom Border**. Make 2 **Outer Top/Bottom Borders**.

4. To determine length of **outer top/bottom borders**, measure *width* across center of quilt top center (including added borders). Trim **outer top/bottom borders** the determined length. Matching centers and corners, sew **outer top/bottom borders** to quilt top center.

COMPLETING THE QUILT

1. Follow **Quilting**, page 68, to mark, layer, and quilt as desired. Our quilt is machine quilted with meandering loops and free-motion dragonflies.

2. Follow **Binding**, page 73, to bind quilt using **binding strips**.

Quilt Top Diagram

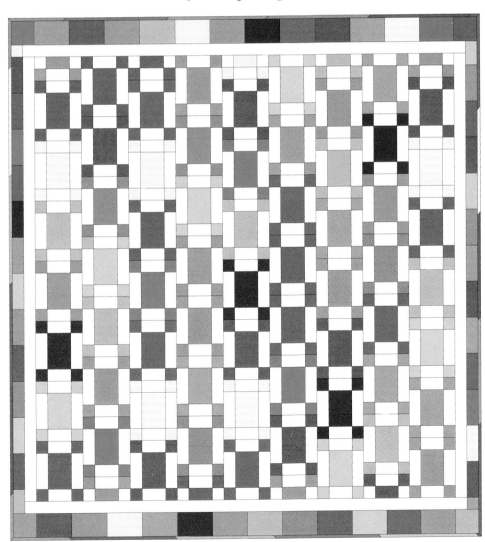

Buttermints

Finished Quilt Size: 54½" x 54½" (138 cm x 138 cm)
Finished Block Size: 9" x 9" (23 cm x 23 cm)

Yardage Requirements

Yardage is based on 43"/44" (109 cm/112 cm) wide fabric with a "usable" width of 40" (102 cm) after trimming selvages and shrinkage.

2⅝ yds (2.4 m) yellow floral print fabric
⅝ yd (57 cm) of yellow mottled print fabric
10" x 16" (25 cm x 41 cm) piece *each* of 13 assorted print fabrics
3½ yds (3.2 m) fabric for backing

You will also need:

63" x 63" (160 cm x 165 cm) square of batting

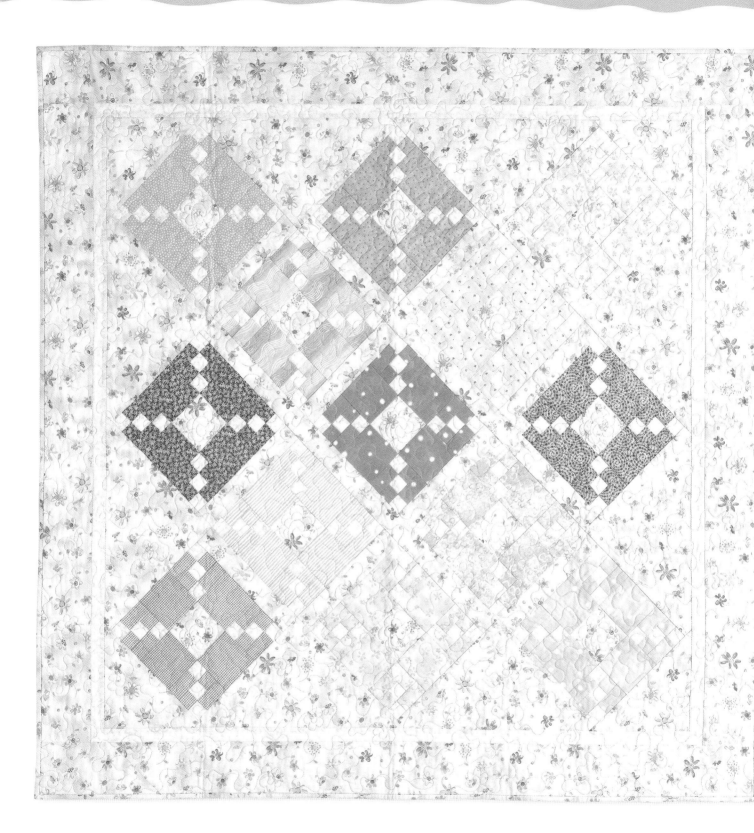

Buttermints

CUTTING OUT THE PIECES

*Follow **Rotary Cutting**, page 66, to cut fabric. All measurements include $^1/_4$" seam allowances.*

From yellow floral print fabric:
- Cut 2 strips $3^1/_2$" wide. From these strips, cut 13 **squares** $3^1/_2$" x $3^1/_2$".
- Cut 5 strips 2" wide. From 3 of these strips, cut 10 **rectangles** 2" x $9^1/_2$". From remaining strips, cut 2 **rectangles** 2" x $30^1/_2$".
- Cut 1 strip $17^1/_4$" wide. From this strip, cut 2 squares $17^1/_4$" x $17^1/_4$". Cut each square twice diagonally to make 8 **setting triangles**.
- Cut 1 strip $8^3/_8$" wide. From this strip, cut 2 squares $8^3/_8$" x $8^3/_8$". Cut each square once diagonally to make 4 **corner setting triangles**.
- Cut 6 **strips** $4^1/_2$" wide.
- Cut 6 **binding strips** $2^1/_4$" wide.

From yellow mottled print fabric:
- Cut 13 strips $1^1/_2$" wide. From 8 of these strips, cut 13 **rectangles** $1^1/_2$" x 13" and 13 **rectangles** $1^1/_2$" x 7". Leave 5 **strips** uncut.

From *each* assorted print fabric:
- Cut 4 **squares** $3^1/_2$" x $3^1/_2$".
- Cut 1 **rectangle** $2^1/_2$" x 13".
- Cut 2 **rectangles** $1^1/_2$" x 7".

ASSEMBLING THE BLOCKS

*Follow **Piecing**, page 67, and **Pressing**, page 68. Use a $^1/_4$" seam allowance throughout. Measurements given throughout assembly include outer seam allowances. Use 1 set of matching fabric pieces to make each Block.*

1. Sew 1 assorted print **rectangle** $2^1/_2$" x 13" and 1 yellow mottled print **rectangle** $1^1/_2$" x 13" together to make **Strip Set A**. Cut across Strip Set A at $1^1/_2$" intervals to make 8 **Unit 1's**. Unit 1 should measure $1^1/_2$" x $3^1/_2$".

Strip Set A   **Unit 1** (make 8)

$1^1/_2$

2. Sew 2 assorted print **rectangles** $1^1/_2$" x 7" and 1 yellow mottled print **rectangle** $1^1/_2$" x 7" together to make **Strip Set B**. Cut across Strip Set B at $1^1/_2$" intervals to make 4 **Unit 2's**. Unit 2 should measure $1^1/_2$" x $3^1/_2$".

Strip Set B   **Unit 2** (make 4)

$1^1/_2$

3. Sew 2 **Unit 1's** and 1 **Unit 2** together to make **Unit 3**. Make 4 **Unit 3's**. Unit 3 should measure $3^1/_2$" x $3^1/_2$".

Unit 3 (make 4)

4. Sew 2 **Unit 3's** and 1 assorted print **square** $3^1/_2$" x $3^1/_2$" together to make **Unit 4**. Make 2 **Unit 4's**. Unit 4 should measure $9^1/_2$" x $3^1/_2$".

Unit 4 (make 2)

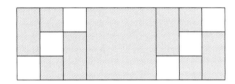

5. Sew 2 assorted print **squares** $3^1/_2$" x $3^1/_2$" and 1 yellow floral print **square** $3^1/_2$" x $3^1/_2$" together to make **Unit 5**. Unit 5 should measure $9^1/_2$" x $3^1/_2$".

Unit 5

6. Sew 2 **Unit 4's** and 1 **Unit 5** together to make **Block**. Make 13 **Blocks**. Block should measure $9^1/_2$" x $9^1/_2$".

Block (make 13)

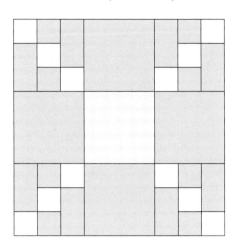

ASSEMBLING THE QUILT TOP CENTER
*Refer to **Assembly Diagram**, page 32.*

1. Sew 1 **Block** and 1 yellow floral 2" x $9^1/_2$" **rectangle** together to make **Unit 6**. Make 2 **Unit 6's**. Unit 6 should measure $9^1/_2$" x 11".

Unit 6 (make 2)

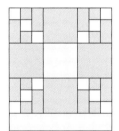

. Aligning right angles of triangles with yellow floral rectangle on Unit 6, sew 1 **Unit 6** and 2 **setting triangles** together to make **Row 1**. Make 2 **Row 1's**.

. Sew 3 **Blocks** and 2 yellow floral 2" x 9$^1/_2$" **rectangles** together to make **Unit 7**. Make 2 **Unit 7's**. Unit 7 should measure 30$^1/_2$" x 9$^1/_2$".

Unit 7 (make 2)

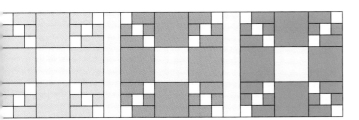

. Sew 1 **Unit 7** and 1 yellow floral 2" x 30$^1/_2$" **rectangle** together to make **Unit 8**. Make 2 **Unit 8's**. Unit 8 should measure 30$^1/_2$" x 11".

Unit 8 (make 2)

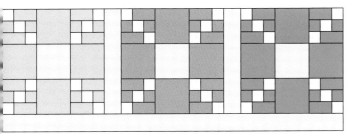

. Aligning right angles of triangles with yellow floral rectangle on Unit 8, sew 1 **Unit 8** and 2 **setting triangles** together to make **Row 2**. Make 2 **Row 2's**.

6. Sew 5 **Blocks** and 4 yellow floral 2" x 9$^1/_2$" **rectangles** together to make **Row 3**. Row 3 should measure 51$^1/_2$" x 9$^1/_2$".

7. Sew Rows 1-3 together in diagonal rows. Sew 1 **corner setting triangle** to each corner to make **Quilt Top Center**. Trim Quilt Top Center to a 44" x 44" square.

ADDING THE BORDERS

Inner Borders

1. Using diagonal seams (**Fig. 1**), sew yellow mottled print **strips** together end to end to make 1 continuous **inner border strip**.

Fig. 1

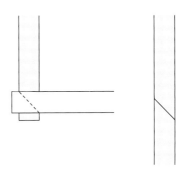

2. To determine length of **inner side borders**, measure *length* across center of quilt top center. From continuous inner border strip, cut 2 **inner side borders** the determined length. Matching centers and corners, sew **inner side borders** to quilt top center.

3. To determine length of **inner top/bottom borders**, measure *width* across center of quilt top center (including added borders). From continuous inner border strip, cut 2 **inner top/bottom borders** the determined length. Matching centers and corners, sew **inner top/bottom borders** to quilt top center.

Outer Borders

1. Using diagonal seams (**Fig. 1**), sew yellow floral **strips** together end to end to make 1 continuous **outer border strip**.
2. Using continuous outer border strip, repeat **Inner Borders**, page 31, Steps 1-3, to attach outer borders.

1. Follow **Quilting**, page 68, to mark, layer, and quilt as desired. Our quilt is machine quilted with a meandering flower design.
2. Follow **Binding**, page 73, to bind quilt using **binding strips**.

Assembly Diagram

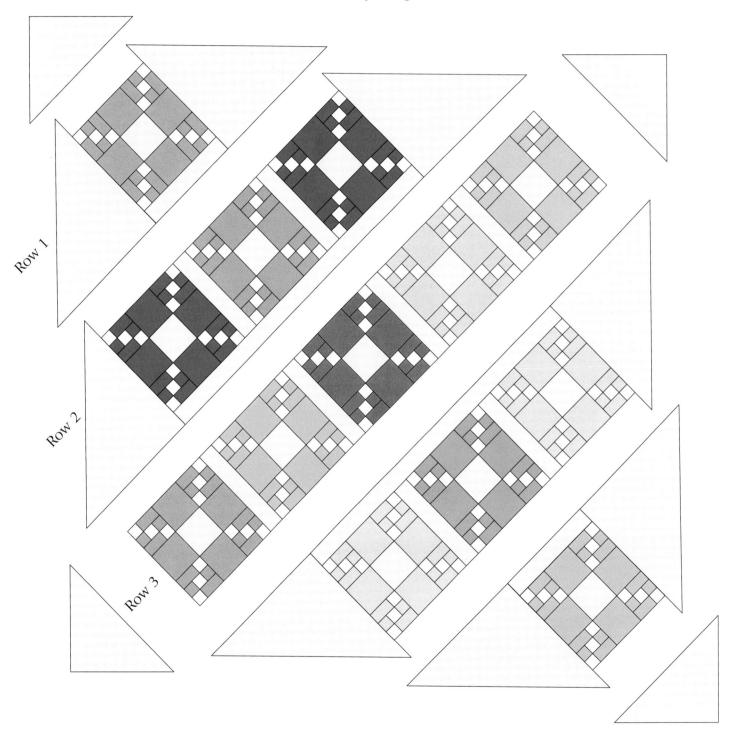

Row 1

Row 2

Row 3

Quilt Top Diagram

Star
Search

Finished Quilt Size: 68¹/₂" x 68¹/₂" (174 cm x 174 cm)
Finished Block Size: 6¹/₈" x 6¹/₈" (16 cm x 16 cm)

Yardage Requirements

Yardage is based on 43"/44" (109 cm/112 cm) wide fabric with a "usable" width of 40" (102 cm) after trimming selvages and shrinkage.

- ¹/₈ yd (11 cm) **each** of 20 or more assorted print fabrics
- 3¹/₂ yds (3.2 m) white solid fabric
- 1 yd (91 cm) yellow print fabric
- 4³/₈ yds (4 m) of fabric for backing

You will also need:

77" x 77" (196 cm x 196 cm) square of batting

Star Search

CUTTING OUT THE PIECES

*Follow **Rotary Cutting**, page 66, to cut fabric. All measurements include $^1/_4$" seam allowances.*

From assorted print fabrics:
- Cut 200 **squares** 4" x 4".

From white solid fabric:
- Cut 17 strips $6^5/_8$" wide. From these strips, cut 100 **squares** $6^5/_8$" x $6^5/_8$".

From yellow print fabric:
- Cut 7 **strips** $1^1/_8$" wide.
- Cut 1 strip 3" wide. From this strip, cut 4 **squares** 3" x 3".
- Cut 8 **binding strips** $2^1/_4$" wide.

ASSEMBLING THE BLOCKS

*Follow **Piecing**, page 67, and **Pressing**, page 68. Measurements given throughout assembly include outer seam allowances. Use a $^1/_4$" seam allowance throughout.*

1. Draw a diagonal line (corner to corner) on wrong side of each 4" print **square**. Draw another diagonal line $^1/_2$" away from first drawn line (**Fig. 1**).

Fig. 1

2. With right sides together, place a marked **square** on two opposite corners of a $6^5/_8$" white **square**. Stitch along each drawn line (**Fig. 2**).

Fig. 2

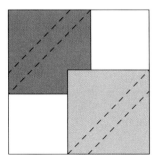

3. Cut through the center of the two stitching lines (**Fig. 3**). Press open to make 1 **Block** and 2 **Triangle-Squares**. Make 100 **Blocks** and 200 **Triangle-Squares**. Blocks should measure $6^5/8$ x $6^5/8$. Trim Triangle-Squares to 3" x 3". (You will only use 100 of these Triangle-Squares. Save the extras to use on another project.) Set Triangle-Squares aside.

Fig. 3

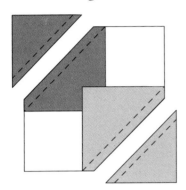

Block (make 100)

Triangle-Squares (make 200)

4. Sew 10 **Blocks** together to make a **Row**. Make 10 **Rows**. Row should measure $61^3/4$" x $6^5/8$".

Row (make 10)

5. Sew **Rows** together to make **Quilt Top Center**. Quilt Top Center should measure $61^3/4$" x $61^3/4$".

ADDING THE BORDERS
Inner Borders
1. Using diagonal seams (**Fig. 4**), sew $1^1/8$" wide yellow print **strips** together end to end to make 1 continuous **inner border strip**.

Fig. 4

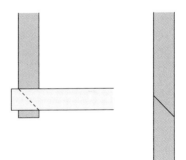

2. To determine length of **inner side borders**, measure *length* across center of quilt top center. From continuous inner border strip, cut 2 **inner side borders** the determined length. Matching centers and corners, sew **inner side borders** to quilt top center.

3. To determine length of **inner top/bottom borders**, measure *width* across center of quilt top center (including added borders). From continuous inner border strips, cut 2 **inner top/bottom borders** the determined length. Matching centers and corners, sew **inner top/bottom borders** to quilt top center.

Outer Borders

1. Sew 25 **Triangle-Squares** together to make **outer border**. Make 4 **outer borders**.
2. Matching centers and corners, sew 1 **outer side border** to each side of quilt top center.

3. Sew a 3" yellow print **square** to each end of remaining **outer borders**.
4. Matching centers and corners, sew **outer top/bottom borders** to Quilt Top Center.

COMPLETING THE QUILT

1. Follow **Quilting**, page 68, to mark, layer, and quilt as desired. Our quilt is machine quilted with a meandering pattern.
2. Follow **Binding**, page 73, to bind quilt using **binding strips**.

Outer Border (make 4)

Pink
Lemonade

Finished Quilt Size: $60^1/_2$" x $69^1/_2$" (154 cm x 177 cm)

Yardage Requirements

Yardage is based on 43"/44" (109 cm/112 cm) wide fabric with a "usable" width of 40" (102 cm) after trimming selvages and shrinkage.

$^3/_4$ yd (69 cm) **each** of 4 pink print fabrics

$^7/_8$ yd (80 cm) **each** of 2 yellow print fabrics

1 yd (91 cm) of pink print fabric for border

$4^3/_8$ yds (4 m) of fabric for backing

$^1/_2$ yd (46 cm) of pink print fabric for binding

You will also need:

69" x 78" (175 cm x 198 cm) square of batting

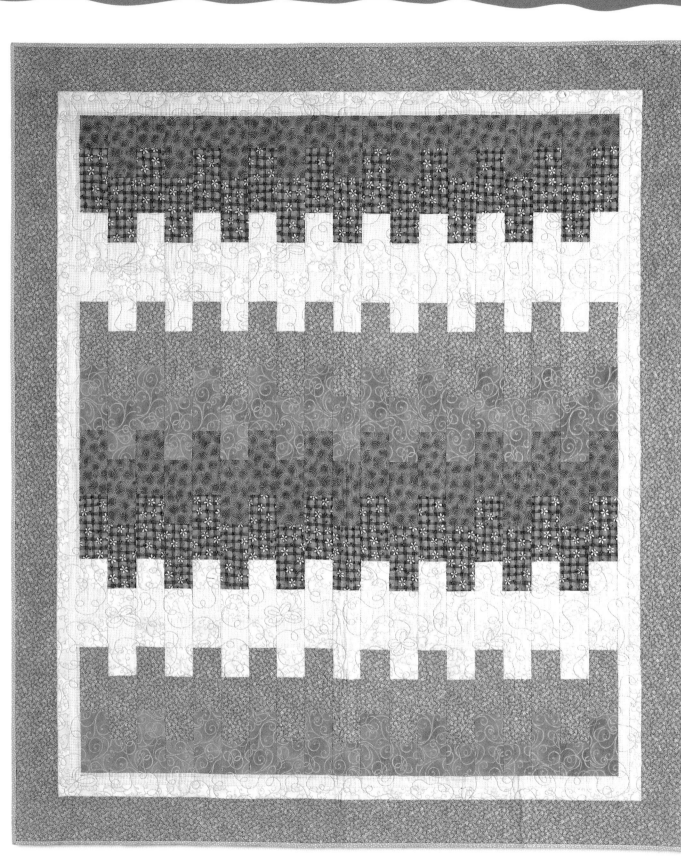

Lemonade

CUTTING OUT THE PIECES

Follow **Rotary Cutting**, page 66, to cut fabric. All measurements include ¹/₄" seam allowances.

From *each* pink print fabric:
- Cut 4 **strips** 6" wide.

From *each* yellow print fabric:
- Cut 6 **strips** 3" wide.
- Cut 6 **border strips** 1¹/₂" wide.

From pink print fabric for border:
- Cut 7 **border strips** 4¹/₂" wide.

From pink print fabric for binding:
- Cut 7 **binding strips** 2¹/₄" wide.

ASSEMBLING THE QUILT TOP CENTER

Follow **Piecing**, page 67, and **Pressing**, page 68. Use ¹/₄" seam allowance throughout. Measurements given throughout assembly include outer seam allowances. Refer to **Quilt Top Diagram**, page 45, for placement.

1. Sew a yellow #1 **strip** to each side of a yellow #2 **strip** to make **Strip Set A**. Make 2 **Strip Set A's**. Press seam allowances toward center strip.

Strip Set A (make 2)

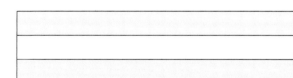

2. Sew a yellow #2 **strip** to each side of a yellow #1 **strip** to make **Strip Set B**. Make 2 **Strip Set B's**. Press seam allowances toward center strip.

Strip Set B (make 2)

3. To make Strip Set C, sew the following strips and strip sets together in this order (top to bottom) pink #1, pink #2, Strip Set A, pink #3, pink #4, pink #1, pink #2, Strip Set B, pink #3, pink #4. Make 2 **Strip Set C's**. Press seam allowances away from yellow Strip Sets. Cut across each **Strip Set C** at 3" intervals to make **Unit 1**. Make 19 **Unit 1's**. Unit 1 should measure 3" x 59$\frac{1}{2}$".

Strip Set C (make 2)   **Unit 1** (make 19)

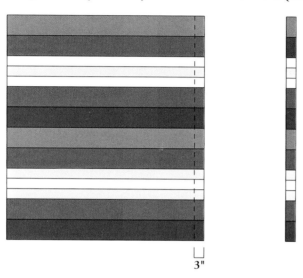

3"

4. Offsetting every other Unit 1 by 2$\frac{1}{2}$", sew **Unit 1's** together along long edges (**Fig. 1**). Trim top and bottom even (**Fig. 2**) to make **Quilt Top Center**. Quilt Top Center should measure 48" x 57".

Fig. 1

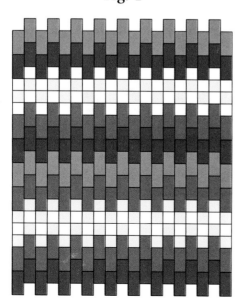

Fig. 2

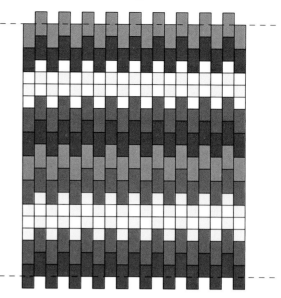

ADDING THE BORDERS
Inner Borders

1. Using diagonal seams (**Fig. 3**), sew yellow #1 **border strips** together end to end to make 1 continuous **inner border strip**.

Fig. 3

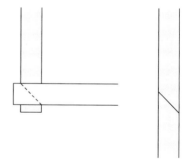

2. To determine length of **inner side borders**, measure *length* across center of quilt top center. From continuous inner border strip, cut 2 **inner side borders** the determined length. Matching centers and corners, sew **inner side borders** to quilt top center.

3. To determine length of **inner top/bottom borders**, measure *width* across center of quilt top center (including added borders). From continuous inner border strip, cut 2 **inner top/bottom borders** the determined length. Matching centers and corners, sew **inner top/bottom borders** to quilt top center.

Middle Borders

. Using yellow #2 **border strips**, repeat **Inner Borders**, page 44, Steps 1-3, to attach middle borders.

Outer Borders

. Using pink **border strips**, repeat **Inner Borders**, page 44, Steps 1-3, to attach outer borders.

COMPLETING THE QUILT

1. Follow **Quilting**, page 68, to mark, layer, and quilt as desired. Our quilt is machine quilted with a meandering loop pattern.
2. Follow **Binding**, page 73, to bind quilt using **binding strips**.

Quilt Top Diagram

$\mathcal{P}$enny Candy

Finished Quilt Size: 81" x 89" (206 cm x 226 cm)
Finished Block Size: 8" x 8" (20 cm x 20 cm)

Yardage Requirements

Yardage is based on 43"/44" (109 cm/112 cm) wide fabric with a "usable" width of 40" (102 cm) after trimming selvages and shrinkage.

  24 assorted print fat quarters*
  $3^1/_4$ yds (3 m) white print fabric
  2 yds (1.8 m) purple print fabric
  $7^1/_2$ yds (6.9 m) of fabric for backing

You will also need:

  89" x 97" (226 cm x 246 cm) square of batting

  *A fat quarter is approximately 18" x 22"
   (46 cm x 56 cm).

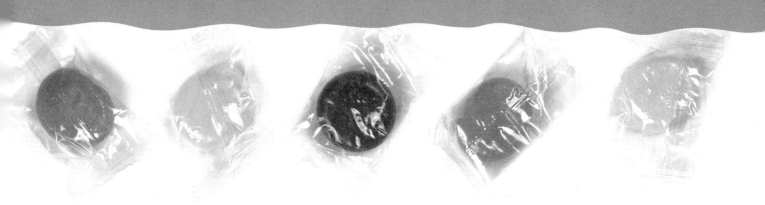

Penny Candy

CUTTING OUT THE PIECES

*Follow **Rotary Cutting**, page 66, to cut fabric. All measurements include ¹/₄" seam allowances.*

From *each* assorted print fat quarter:
- Cut 12 **squares** 2¹/₂" x 2¹/₂".
- Cut 3 **squares** 4⁷/₈" x 4⁷/₈".

From *remaining* scraps of assorted fat quarters:
- Cut enough 2¹/₄" wide **binding strips** of various lengths to equal 360" when sewn together end to end.

From white print fabric:
- Cut 18 strips 2¹/₂" wide. From these strips, cut 288 **squares** 2¹/₂" x 2¹/₂".
- Cut 9 strips 4⁷/₈" wide". From these strips, cut 72 **squares** 4⁷/₈" x 4⁷/₈".
- Cut 8 **border strips** 2" wide.

From purple print fabric:
- Cut 8 **border strips** 2¹/₂" wide.
- Cut 9 **border strips** 5" wide.

ASSEMBLING THE BLOCKS

*Follow **Piecing**, page 67, and **Pressing**, page 68. Use a ¹/₄" seam allowance throughout. Measurements given throughout assembly include outer seam allowances. Each Block consists of 2 matching Triangle-Squares and 2 matching Unit 2's.*

1. Draw a diagonal line (corner to corner) on wrong side of each 4⁷/₈" white print **square**. With right sides together, place a white print **square** on top of a 4⁷/₈" assorted print **square**. Stitch seam ¹/₄" from each side of drawn line (**Fig. 1**).

Fig. 1

2. Cut along drawn line and press open to make 2 **Triangle-Squares**. Make 72 sets of 2 matching **Triangle-Squares**. Triangle-Squares should measure 4¹/₂" x 4¹/₂".

Triangle-Squares (make 72 sets of 2 matching)

3. Sew a $2^1/_2$" white print **square** and a $2^1/_2$" assorted print **square** together to make **Unit 1**. Make 72 sets of 4 matching **Unit 1's**. Unit 1 should measure $2^1/_2$" x $4^1/_2$".

Unit 1 (make 72 sets of 4 matching)

4. Sew 2 matching **Unit 1's** together to make **Unit 2**. Make 72 sets of 2 matching Unit **2's**. Unit 2 should measure $4^1/_2$" x $4^1/_2$".

Unit 2 (make 72 sets of 2 matching)

5. Sew 2 matching **Triangle-Squares** and 2 matching **Unit 2's** together to make **Block A**. Make 36 **Block A's**. Block A should measure $8^1/_2$" x $8^1/_2$".

Block A (make 36)

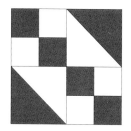

6. Sew 2 matching **Triangle-Squares** and 2 matching **Unit 2's** together to make **Block B**. Make 36 **Block B's**. Block B should measure $8^1/_2$" x $8^1/_2$".

Block B (make 36)

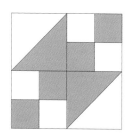

ASSEMBLING THE QUILT TOP CENTER
*Refer to **Quilt Top Diagram**, page 51, for placement.*

1. Alternating Blocks, sew 4 **Block A's** and 4 **Block B's** together to make **Row**. Make 9 **Rows**. Row should measure $64^1/_2$" x $8^1/_2$".

Row

2. Rotating every other Row, sew **Rows** together to make **Quilt Top Center**. Quilt Top Center should measure $64^1/_2$" x $72^1/_2$".

ADDING THE BORDERS
Inner Borders

1. Using diagonal seams (**Fig. 2**), sew $2^1/_2$" purple **border strips** together end to end to make 1 continuous **inner border strip**.

Fig. 2

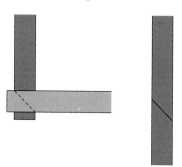

2. To determine length of **inner side borders**, measure *length* across center of quilt top center. From continuous inner border strip, cut 2 **inner side borders** the determined length. Matching centers and corners, sew **inner side borders** to quilt top center.

3. To determine length of **inner top/bottom borders**, measure *width* across center of quilt top center (including added borders). From continuous inner border strip, cut 2 **inner top/bottom borders** the determined length. Matching centers and corners, sew **inner top/bottom borders** to quilt top center.

Middle Borders

Using white print **border strips**, repeat **Inner Borders**, page 50, Steps 1-3, to attach middle borders.

Outer Borders

Using 5" purple print **border strips**, repeat **Inner Borders**, page 50, Steps 1-3, to attach outer borders.

COMPLETING THE QUILT

1. Follow **Quilting**, page 68, to mark, layer, and quilt as desired. Our quilt is machine quilted with a meandering loop and heart pattern.
2. Follow **Binding**, page 73, to bind quilt.

Quilt Top Diagram

Petal Pushers

Finished Quilt Size: 73" x 73" (185 cm x 185 cm)
Finished Block Size: $8^{1}/_{8}$" x $8^{1}/_{8}$" (21 cm x 21 cm)

Yardage Requirements

Yardage is based on 43"/44" (109 cm/112 cm) wide fabric with a "usable" width of 40" (102 cm) after trimming selvages and shrinkage.

- $2^{1}/_{2}$ yds (2.3 m) **total** of assorted print fabrics
- $^{5}/_{8}$ yd (57 cm) yellow print fabric
- $3^{7}/_{8}$ yds (3.5 m) white solid fabric
- 1 yd (91 cm) **total** of assorted green print fabrics
- $4^{1}/_{2}$ yds (4.1 m) of fabric for backing
- $^{5}/_{8}$ yd (57 cm) of fabric for binding

You will also need:

- 81" x 81" (206 cm x 206 cm) square of batting

Petal Pusher

CUTTING OUT THE PIECES

Follow **Rotary Cutting**, *page 66, to cut fabric. All measurements include* $^1/_4$" *seam allowances.*

From assorted print fabrics:
- Cut 49 sets of 4 matching **squares** 4" x 4" (**A**).

From yellow print fabric:
- Cut 5 **strips** $1^5/_8$" wide (**B**).
- Cut 3 **strips** $3^7/_8$" wide (**C**).

From white solid fabric:
- Cut 11 **strips** $2^7/_8$" wide (**D**).
- Cut 27 strips $1^3/_4$" wide. From these strips, cut 584 **squares** $1^3/_4$" x $1^3/_4$" (**E**).
- Cut 28 strips $1^5/_8$" wide. From 11 of these strips, cut 42 **short sashings** $1^5/_8$" x $8^5/_8$" (**F**). Leave 17 strips (**G**) uncut.

From assorted green print fabrics:
- Cut 92 **squares** $3^1/_2$" x $3^1/_2$" (**H**).

From fabric for binding:
- Cut 8 **binding strips** $2^1/_4$" wide (**I**).

ASSEMBLING THE BLOCKS

Follow **Piecing**, *page 67, and* **Pressing**, *page 68. Measurements given throughout assembly include outer seam allowances. Use a* $^1/_4$" *seam allowance throughout.*

1. Draw a diagonal line (corner to corner) on wrong side of each **square** (**E**). With right sides together, place a **square** (**E**) on opposite corners of a **square** (**A**). Stitch seam on marked line. Set aside remaining **squares** (**E**).
2. Trim seam allowance to $^1/_4$" (**Fig. 1**) and press open to make **Unit 1**. Unit 1 should measure 4" x 4". Make 49 sets of 4 matching **Unit 1's**.

Fig. 1

Unit 1 (make 49 sets of 4 matching)

3. Sew 1 **strip** (B) and 1 **strip** (D) together to make **Strip Set A**. Make 5 **Strip Set A's**. Cut across Strip Set A's at $1^5/_8$" intervals to make **Unit 2**. Unit 2 should measure $1^5/_8$" x 4". Make 98 **Unit 2's**.

Strip Set A (make 5)   **Unit 2** (make 98)

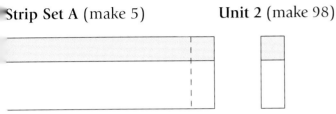

$1^5/_8$

4. Sew 1 **strip** (D) to each side of 1 **strip** (C) to make **Strip Set B**. Make 3 **Strip Set B's**. Cut across Strip Set B's at $1^5/_8$" intervals to make **Unit 3**. Unit 3 should measure $1^5/_8$" x $8^5/_8$". Make 49 **Unit 3's**.

Strip Set B (make 3)   **Unit 3** (make 49)

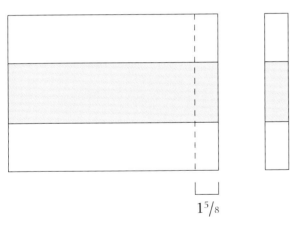

$1^5/_8$

5. Sew 2 matching **Unit 1's** and 1 **Unit 2** together to make **Unit 4**. Unit 4 should measure $8^5/_8$" x 4". Make 98 **Unit 4's**.

Unit 4 (make 98)

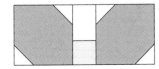

6. Sew 1 **Unit 3** and 2 matching **Unit 4's** together to make **Flower Block**. Flower Block should measure $8^5/_8$" x $8^5/_8$". Make 49 **Flower Blocks**.

Flower Block (make 49)

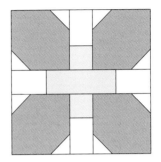

ASSEMBLING THE QUILT TOP CENTER

*Refer to **Quilt Top Diagram**, page 57, for placement.*
1. Sew 7 **Flower Blocks** and 6 **short sashings** (F) together to make a **Row**. A Row should measure $64^1/_8$" x $8^5/_8$". Make 7 **Rows**.

Row (make 7)

2. Using diagonal seams (**Fig. 2**), sew 10 **strips** (G) together end to end to make 1 continuous length. From this length, cut 6 **long sashings** $1^5/_8$" x $64^1/_8$".

Fig. 2

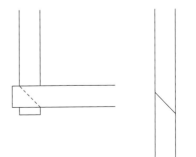

3. Sew 7 **Rows** and 6 **long sashings** together to make **Quilt Top Center**. The Quilt Top Center should measure 64$\frac{1}{8}$" x 64$\frac{1}{8}$".

Inner Borders

1. Using diagonal seams (**Fig. 2**), sew 7 **strips** (**G**) together end to end to make 1 continuous inner border strip.
2. To determine length of **inner side borders**, measure *length* across center of quilt top center. From continuous inner border strip, cut 2 **inner side borders** the determined length. Matching centers and corners, sew **inner side borders** to quilt top center.
3. To determine length of **inner top/bottom borders**, measure *width* across center of quilt top center (including added borders). From continuous inner border strip, cut 2 **inner top/bottom borders** the determined length. Matching centers and corners, sew **inner top/bottom borders** to quilt top center.

Outer Borders

1. With right sides together, place a white **square** (**E**) on opposite corners of a **square** (**H**). Stitch seam on marked line.
2. Trim seam allowance to $\frac{1}{4}$" (**Fig. 3**) and press open to make **Leaf Block**. Leaf Block should measure 3$\frac{1}{2}$" x 3$\frac{1}{2}$". Make 92 **Leaf Blocks**.

Fig. 3

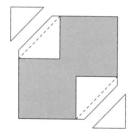

Leaf Block (make 92)

3. With right sides together, place a white **square** (**E**) on each remaining corner of a **Leaf Block**. Stitch seam on marked line.
4. Trim seam allowance to $\frac{1}{4}$" (**Fig. 4**) and press open to make **Cornerstone Block**. Cornerstone Block should measure 3$\frac{1}{2}$" x 3$\frac{1}{2}$". Make 4 **Cornerstone Blocks**.

Fig. 4

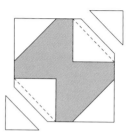

Cornerstone Block (make 4)

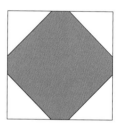

5. Sew 22 **Leaf Blocks** together to make **Outer Border**. Adjust Outer Border length to measure 66$\frac{3}{8}$" long by taking smaller or larger seam allowances as needed. Make 4 **Outer Borders**.
6. Matching centers and corners, sew 1 **Outer Border** to each side of quilt top.
7. Sew a **Cornerstone Block** to each end of remaining **Outer Borders**.
8. Matching centers and corners, sew 1 **Outer Border** to top and bottom of quilt top.

. Follow **Quilting**, page 68, to mark, layer, and quilt as desired. Our quilt is machine quilted with meandering loops and free-motion dragonflies.

2. Follow **Binding**, page 73, to bind quilt using **binding strips (I)**.

Quilt Top Diagram

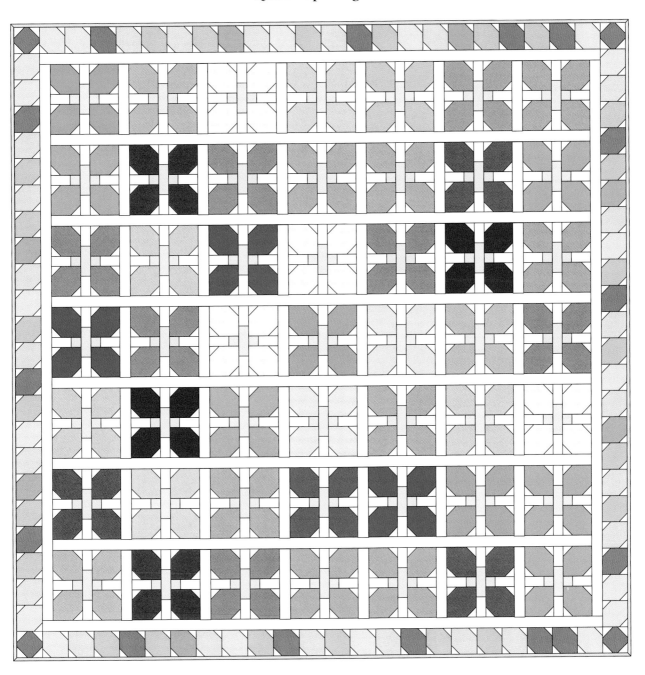

Orange Slices

Finished Quilt Size: 67" x 67" (170 cm x 170 cm)
Finished Block Size: 13" x 13" (33 cm x 33 cm)

Yardage Requirements

Yardage is based on 43"/44" (109 cm/112 cm) wide fabric with a "usable" width of 40" (102 cm) after trimming selvages and shrinkage.

- $2\frac{1}{2}$ yds (2.3 m) **total** of assorted orange print fabrics
- $3\frac{3}{8}$ yds (3.1 m) floral print fabric
- $\frac{1}{2}$ yd (46 cm) yellow dot print fabric
- $4\frac{1}{4}$ yds (3.9 m) of fabric for backing
- $\frac{1}{2}$ yd (46 cm) of fabric for binding

You will also need:

75" x 75" (191 cm x 191 cm) square of batting

Orange Slices

CUTTING OUT THE PIECES

Follow **Rotary Cutting**, page 66, to cut fabric. Borders include an extra 4" of length for "insurance," and will be trimmed after assembling quilt top center. All measurements include $^1/_4$" seam allowances.

From assorted orange print fabrics:
- Cut 32 sets of 1 **square** $7^3/_8$" x $7^3/_8$"and 2 **rectangles** 2" x 7". (Each set should be cut from 1 fabric.)
- Cut 8 **squares** $4^3/_8$" x $4^3/_8$".

From floral print fabric:
- Cut 4 *lengthwise* borders $7^1/_2$" x $56^1/_2$".
- Cut 7 strips $7^3/_8$" wide. From these strips, cut 32 **squares** $7^3/_8$" x $7^3/_8$".

From yellow dot print fabric:
- Cut 4 strips 2" wide. From these strips, cut 64 **squares** 2" x 2".
- Cut 1 strip $4^3/_8$" wide. From this strip, cut 8 **squares** $4^3/_8$" x $4^3/_8$".

From fabric for binding:
- Cut 7 **binding strips** $2^1/_4$" wide.

ASSEMBLING THE BLOCKS

*Follow **Piecing**, page 67, and **Pressing**, page 68. Use a $^1/_4$" seam allowance throughout. Measurements given throughout assembly include outer seam allowances.*

Orange Slice Blocks

1. Draw a diagonal line (corner to corner) on wrong side of each $7^3/_8$" floral **square**. With right sides together, place a floral **square** on top of $7^3/_8$" orange **square**. Stitch seam $^1/_4$" from each side of drawn line (**Fig. 1**).

Fig. 1

2. Cut along drawn line and press open to make 2 **Triangle-Square A's**. Triangle-Square A should measure 7" x 7". Make 64 **Triangle-Square A's**.

Triangle-Square A's (make 64)

3. With orange print in lower right corner, cut Triangle-Square A's into 4 **segments** 1³/₄" x 7" (**Fig. 2**). Set segments aside.

Fig. 2

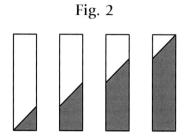

4. Draw a diagonal line (corner to corner) on wrong side of each 2" yellow dot **square**. With right sides together, place a yellow dot **square** on one end of a 2" x 7" orange **rectangle**. Stitch along drawn line (**Fig. 3**).

Fig. 3

5. Trim seam allowance to ¹/₄" and press open to make **Unit 1**. Make 64 **Unit 1's**. Unit 1 should measure 2" x 7".

Unit 1 (make 64)

6. Arrange and sew matching segments and Unit 1's together as shown to make **Unit 2**. Make 64 **Unit 2's**. Unit 2 should measure 7" x 7".

Unit 2

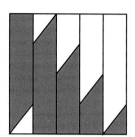

7. Sew 4 different **Unit 2's** together to make **Orange Slice Block**. Make 16 **Orange Slice Blocks**. Orange Slice Block should measure 13¹/₂" x 13¹/₂".

Orange Slice Block (make 16)

nwheel Blocks

Draw a diagonal line (corner to corner) on wrong side of each $4^3/8$" yellow dot **square**. With right sides together, place a yellow dot **square** on top of a $4^3/8$" orange **square**. Stitch seam $1/4$" from each side of drawn line (**Fig. 4**).

Fig. 4

Cut along drawn line and press open to make 2 **Triangle-Square B's**. Make 16 **Triangle-Square B's**. Triangle-Square B should measure 4" x 4".

Triangle-Square B's (make 16)

Sew 4 **Triangle-Square B's** together to make a **Pinwheel Block**. Make 4 **Pinwheel Blocks**. Pinwheel Block should measure $7^1/2$" x $7^1/2$".

Pinwheel Block

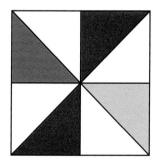

ASSEMBLING THE QUILT TOP CENTER

*Refer to **Quilt Top Diagram**, page 64, for placement.*

1. Sew 4 **Orange Slice Blocks** together to make a **Row**. Row should measure $52^1/2$" x $13^1/2$". Make 4 **Rows**.
2. Sew **Rows** together to make **Quilt Top Center**. Quilt Top Center should measure $52^1/2$" x $52^1/2$".

ADDING THE BORDERS

1. To determine length of **side borders**, measure *length* across center of quilt top center. Trim 2 **side borders** to the determined length. Do not sew side borders to quilt top at this time.
2. To determine length of **top/bottom borders**, measure *width* across center of quilt top center. Trim 2 **top/bottom borders** to the determined length. Do not sew top/bottom borders to quilt top at this time.
3. Matching centers and corners, sew **side borders** to Quilt Top Center.
4. Sew 1 **Pinwheel Block** to each end of each **top/bottom border**.
5. Matching centers and corners, sew **top/bottom borders** to Quilt Top Center.

COMPLETING THE QUILT

1. Follow **Quilting**, page 68, to mark, layer, and quilt as desired. Our quilt is machine quilted with a meandering swirl pattern.
2. Follow **Binding**, page 73, to bind quilt using **binding strips**.

Quilt Top Diagram

General Instructions

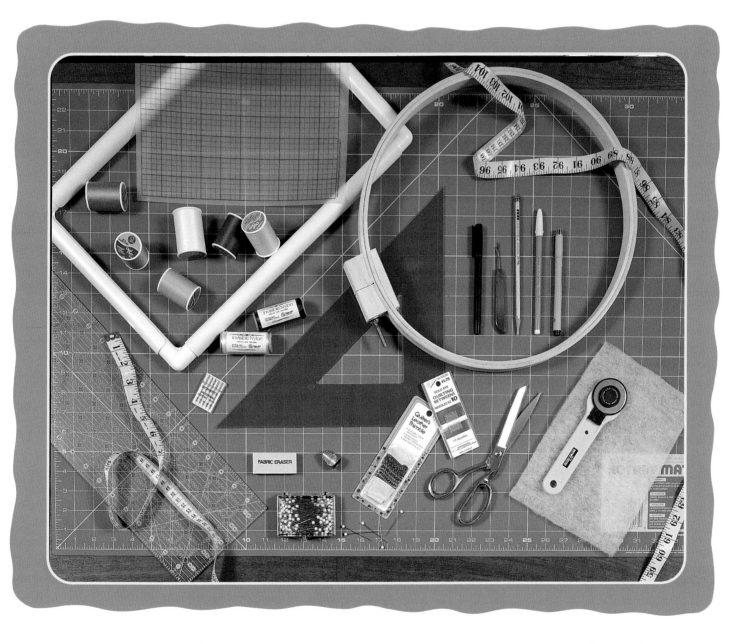

To make your quilting easier and more enjoyable, we encourage you to carefully read all of the general instructions, study the color photographs, and familiarize yourself with the individual project instructions before beginning a project.

FABRICS

SELECTING FABRICS

Choose high-quality, medium-weight 100% cotton fabrics. All-cotton fabrics hold a crease better, fray less, and are easier to quilt than cotton/polyester blends.

Yardage requirements listed for each project are based on 43"/44" wide fabric with a "usable" width of 40" after shrinkage and trimming selvages. Actual usable width will probably vary slightly from fabric to fabric. Our recommended yardage lengths should be adequate for occasional re-squaring of fabric when many cuts are required.

PREPARING FABRICS

We recommend that all fabrics be washed, dried, and pressed before cutting. If fabrics are not pre-washed, washing the finished quilt will cause shrinkage and give it a more "antiqued" look and feel. Bright and dark colors, which may run, should always be washed before cutting. After washing and drying fabric, fold lengthwise with wrong sides together and matching selvages.

ROTARY CUTTING

Rotary cutting has brought speed and accuracy to quiltmaking by allowing quilters to easily cut strips of fabric and then cut those strips into smaller pieces.

- Place fabric on work surface with fold closest to you.

- Square left edge of fabric using rotary cutter and rulers (**Figs. 1 – 2**).

Fig. 1

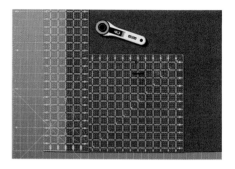

Fig. 2

- Cut all strips from the selvage-to-selvage width of the fabric unless otherwise indicated in project instructions.

- To cut each strip required for a project, place ruler over cut edge of fabric, aligning desired marking on ruler with cut edge; make cut (**Fig. 3**).

Fig. 3

When cutting several strips from a single piece of fabric, it is important to make sure that cuts remain at a perfect right angle to the fold; square fabric as needed.

PIECING
Precise cutting, followed by accurate piecing, will ensure that all pieces of quilt top fit together well.

HAND PIECING

Use ruler and sharp fabric marking pencil to draw all seam lines and transfer any alignment markings onto back of cut pieces.

Matching right sides, pin two pieces together, using pins to mark corners.

Use Running Stitch to sew pieces together along drawn line, backstitching at beginning and end of seam.

Do not extend stitches into seam allowances.

Run five or six stitches onto needle before pulling needle through fabric.

- To add stability, backstitch every $3/4$" to 1".

MACHINE PIECING

- Set sewing machine stitch length for approximately 11 stitches per inch.

- Use neutral-colored general-purpose sewing thread (not quilting thread) in needle and in bobbin.

- An accurate $1/4$" seam allowance is *essential*. Presser feet that are $1/4$" wide are available for most sewing machines.

- When piecing, always place pieces right sides together and match raw edges; pin if necessary.

- Chain piecing saves time and will usually result in more accurate piecing.

- Trim away points of seam allowances that extend beyond edges of sewn pieces.

Sewing Strip Sets
When there are several strips to assemble into a strip set, first sew strips together into pairs, then sew pairs together to form strip set. To help avoid distortion, sew seams in opposite directions (**Fig. 4**). Take special care not to stretch outer strips.

Fig. 4

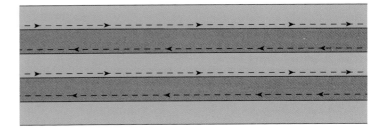

Sewing Across Seam Intersections
When sewing across intersection of two seams, place pieces right sides together and match seams exactly, making sure seam allowances are pressed in opposite directions (**Fig. 5**).

Fig. 5

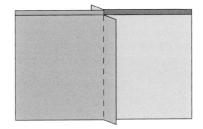

Sewing Sharp Points

To ensure sharp points when joining triangular or diagonal pieces, stitch across the center of the "X" (shown in pink) formed on wrong side by previous seams (**Fig. 6**).

Fig. 6

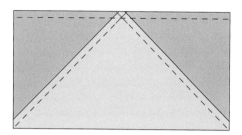

PRESSING

- Use steam iron set on "Cotton" for all pressing.

- Press after sewing each seam.

- Traditionally, seam allowances have been pressed to one side, usually toward the darker fabric. However, with better fabrics, thread, and machine piecing, pressing seams open has become more commonplace. Pressing seams open may reduce bulk and make points sharper.

- To prevent dark fabric seam allowance from showing through light fabric, trim darker seam allowance slightly narrower than lighter seam allowance.

- To press long seams, such as those in long strip sets, without curving or other distortion, lay strips across width of the ironing board.

QUILTING

*Quilting holds the three layers (top, batting, and backing) of the quilt together and can be done by hand or machine. Because marking, layering, and quilting are interrelated and may be done in different orders depending on circumstances, please read entire **Quilting** section, pages 68 – 73, before beginning project.*

TYPES OF QUILTING DESIGNS

In the Ditch Quilting

Quilting along seamlines or along edges of appliquéd pieces is called "in the ditch" quilting. This type of quilting should be done on side **opposite** seam allowance and does not have to be marked.

Outline Quilting

Quilting a consistent distance, usually $1/4$", from seam or appliqué is called "outline" quilting. Outline quilting may be marked, or $1/4$" masking tape may be placed along seamlines for quilting guide. (Do not leave tape on quilt longer than necessary, since it may leave an adhesive residue.)

Motif Quilting

Quilting a design, such as a feathered wreath, is called "motif" quilting. This type of quilting should be marked before basting quilt layers together.

Echo Quilting

Quilting that follows the outline of an appliquéd or pieced design with two or more parallel lines is called "echo" quilting. This type of quilting does not need to be marked.

Channel Quilting

Quilting with straight, parallel lines is called "channel" quilting. This type of quilting may be marked or stitched using a guide.

Crosshatch Quilting

Quilting straight lines in a grid pattern is called "crosshatch" quilting. Lines may be stitched parallel to edges of quilt or stitched diagonally. This type of quilting may be marked or stitched using a guide.

Meandering Quilting

Quilting in random curved lines and swirls is called "meandering" quilting. Quilting lines should not cross or touch each other. This type of quilting does not need to be marked.

Stipple Quilting

Meandering quilting that is very closely spaced is called "stipple" quilting. Stippling will flatten the area quilted and is often stitched in background areas to raise appliquéd or pieced designs. This type of quilting does not need to be marked.

MARKING QUILTING LINES

Quilting lines may be marked using fabric marking pencils, chalk markers, water- or air-soluble pens, or lead pencils.

Simple quilting designs may be marked with chalk or chalk pencil after basting. A small area may be marked, then quilted, before moving to next area to be marked. Intricate designs should be marked before basting using a more durable marker.

Caution: Pressing may permanently set some marks. **Test** different markers **on scrap fabric** to find one that marks clearly and can be thoroughly removed.

A wide variety of pre-cut quilting stencils, as well as entire books of quilting patterns, are available. Using a stencil makes it easier to mark intricate or repetitive designs.

To make a stencil from a pattern, center template plastic over pattern and use a permanent marker to trace pattern onto plastic. Use a craft knife with single or double blade to cut channels along traced lines (**Fig. 7**).

Fig. 7

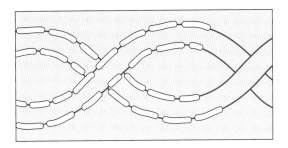

PREPARING THE BACKING

To allow for slight shifting of quilt top during quilting, backing should be approximately 4" larger on all sides, especially for quilts which will be quilted on a long arm machine. Less fabric (2" to 3" larger on all sides) is adequate for quilts which will be hand quilted or quilted on a regular sewing machine. In some cases, this will allow you to avoid purchasing an extra length of fabric. Yardage requirements listed for quilt backings are calculated for 43"/44"w fabric. Using 90"w or 108"w fabric for the backing of a bed-sized quilt may eliminate piecing. To piece a backing using 43"/44"w fabric, use the following instructions.

1. Measure length and width of quilt top; add 8" to each measurement.

2. If determined width is 79" or less, cut backing fabric into two lengths slightly longer than determined **length** measurement. Trim selvages. Place lengths with right sides facing and sew long edges together, forming tube (**Fig. 8**). Match seams and press along one fold (**Fig. 9**). Cut along pressed fold to form single piece (**Fig. 10**).

Fig. 8

Fig. 9

Fig. 10

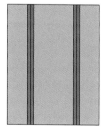

3. If determined width is more than 79", it may require less fabric yardage if the backing is pieced horizontally. Divide determined **length** measurement by 40" to determine how many widths will be needed. Cut required number of widths the determined **width** measurement. Trim selvages. Sew long edges together to form single piece.

4. Trim backing to size determined in Step 1; press seam allowances open.

CHOOSING THE BATTING

The appropriate batting will make quilting easier. For fine hand quilting, choose low-loft batting. All cotton or cotton/polyester blend battings work well for machine quilting because the cotton helps "grip" quilt layers. If quilt is to be tied, a high-loft batting, sometimes called extra-loft or fat batting, may be used to make quilt "fluffy."

Types of batting include cotton, polyester, wool, cotton/polyester blend, cotton/wool blend, and silk.

When selecting batting, refer to package labels for characteristics and care instructions. Batting should be cut same size as prepared backing.

ASSEMBLING THE QUILT

1. Examine wrong side of quilt top closely; trim any seam allowances and clip any threads that may show through front of the quilt. Press quilt top, being careful not to "set" any marked quilting lines.
2. Place backing **wrong** side up on flat surface. Use masking tape to tape edges of backing to surface. Place batting on top of backing fabric. Smooth batting gently, being careful not to stretch or tear. Center quilt top **right** side up on batting.
3. If hand quilting, begin in center and work toward outer edges to hand baste all layers together. Use long stitches and place basting lines approximately 4" apart (**Fig. 11**). Smooth fullness or wrinkles toward outer edges.

Fig. 11

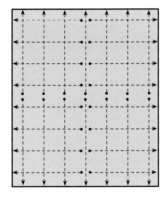

4. If machine quilting, use 1" rustproof safety pins to "pin-baste" all layers together, spacing pins approximately 4" apart. Begin at center and work toward outer edges to secure all layers. If possible, place pins away from areas that will be quilted, although pins may be removed as needed when quilting.

HAND QUILTING

The quilting stitch is a basic running stitch that forms a broken line on quilt top and backing. Stitches on quilt top and backing should be straight and equal in length.

1. Secure center of quilt in hoop or frame. Check quilt top and backing to make sure they are smooth. To help prevent puckers, always begin quilting in the center of quilt and work toward outside edges.
2. Thread needle with 18" - 20" length of quilting thread; knot one end. Using thimble, insert needle into quilt top and batting approximately $\frac{1}{2}$" from quilting line. Bring needle up on quilting line (**Fig. 12**); when knot catches on quilt top, give thread a quick, short pull to "pop" knot through fabric into batting (**Fig. 13**).

Fig. 12	**Fig. 13**

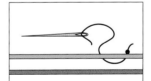
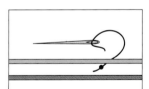

3. Holding needle with sewing hand and placing other hand underneath quilt, use thimble to push tip of needle down through all layers. As soon as needle touches finger underneath, use that finger to push tip of needle only back up through layers to top of quilt. (The amount of needle showing above fabric determines length of quilting stitch.) Referring to **Fig. 14**, rock needle up and down, taking three to six stitches before bringing needle and thread completely through layers. Check back of quilt to make sure stitches are going through all layers. If necessary, make one stitch at a time when quilting through seam allowances or along curves and corners.

Fig. 14

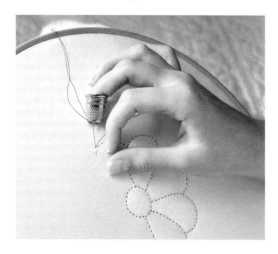

4. At end of thread, knot thread close to fabric and "pop" knot into batting; clip thread close to fabric.
5. Move hoop as often as necessary. Thread may be left dangling and picked up again after returning to that part of quilt.

MACHINE QUILTING METHODS
Use general-purpose thread in bobbin. Do not use quilting thread. Thread the needle of machine with general-purpose thread or transparent monofilament thread to make quilting blend with quilt top fabrics. Use decorative thread, such as a metallic or contrasting-color general-purpose thread, to make quilting lines stand out more.

Straight-Line Quilting
The term "straight-line" is somewhat deceptive, since curves (especially gentle ones) as well as straight lines can be stitched with this technique.
1. Set stitch length for six to ten stitches per inch and attach walking foot to sewing machine.
2. Determine which section of quilt will have longest continuous quilting line, oftentimes area from center top to center bottom. Roll up and secure each edge of quilt to help reduce the bulk, keeping fabrics smooth. Smaller projects may not need to be rolled.
3. Begin stitching on longest quilting line, using very short stitches for the first $1/4$" to "lock" quilting. Stitch across project, using one hand on each side of walking foot to slightly spread fabric and to guide fabric through machine. Lock stitches at end of quilting line.
4. Continue machine quilting, stitching longer quilting lines first to stabilize quilt before moving on to other areas.

ree-Motion Quilting

ree-motion quilting may be free form or may follow a marked pattern.

. Attach darning foot to sewing machine and lower or cover feed dogs.

. Position quilt under darning foot; lower foot. Holding top thread, take a stitch and pull bobbin thread to top of quilt. To "lock" beginning of quilting line, hold top and bobbin threads while making three to five stitches in place.

. Use one hand on each side of darning foot to slightly spread fabric and to move fabric through the machine. Even stitch length is achieved by using smooth, flowing hand motion and steady machine speed. Slow machine speed and fast hand movement will create long stitches. Fast machine speed and slow hand movement will create short stitches. Move quilt sideways, back and forth, in a circular motion, or in a random motion to create desired designs; do not rotate quilt. Lock stitches at end of each quilting line.

BINDING

1. Using diagonal seams (**Fig. 15**), sew binding strips together end to end to make 1 continuous **binding strip**. Trim ends of binding strip square.

Fig. 15

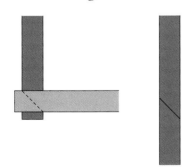

2. Matching wrong sides and raw edges, carefully press binding strip in half lengthwise.

3. Beginning with one end near center on bottom edge of quilt, lay binding around quilt to make sure that seams in binding will not end up at a corner. Adjust placement if necessary. Matching raw edges of binding to raw edge of quilt top, pin binding to right side of quilt along one edge.

4. When you reach the first corner, mark $^1/_4$" from corner of quilt top (**Fig. 16**).

Fig. 16

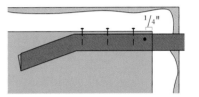

5. Beginning approximately 10" from end of binding and using a $^1/_4$" seam allowance, sew binding to quilt, backstitching at beginning of stitching and at mark (**Fig. 17**). Lift needle out of fabric and clip thread.

Fig. 17

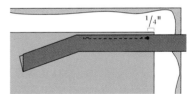

6. Fold binding as shown in **Figs. 18 and** 19 and pin binding to adjacent side, matching raw edges. When you reach the next corner, mark ¹/₄" from edge of quilt top.

Fig. 18

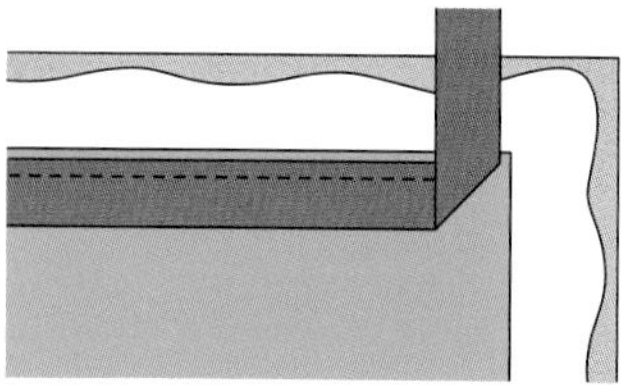

Fig. 19

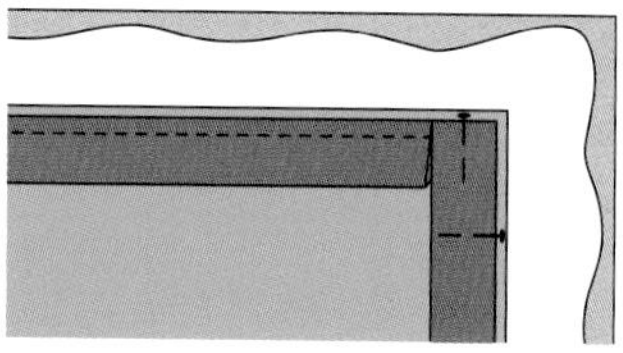

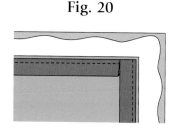

7. Backstitching at edge of quilt top, sew pinned binding to quilt (**Fig. 20**); backstitch when you reach the next mark. Lift needle out of fabric and clip thread.

Fig. 20

8. Continue sewing binding to quilt, stopping approximately 10" from starting point (**Fig. 21**).

Fig. 21

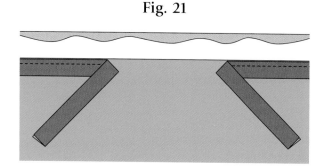

9. Bring beginning and end of binding to center o opening and fold each end back, leaving a ¹/₄" space between folds (**Fig. 22**). Finger-press fold

Fig. 22

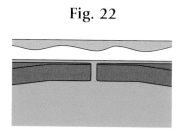

10. Unfold ends of binding and draw a line across wrong side in finger-pressed crease. Draw a line through the lengthwise pressed fold of binding at same spot to create a cross mark. With edge of ruler at marked cross, line up 45° angle marking on ruler with one long side of binding Draw a diagonal line from edge to edge. Repeat on remaining end, making sure that the two lines are angled the same way (**Fig. 23**).

Fig. 23

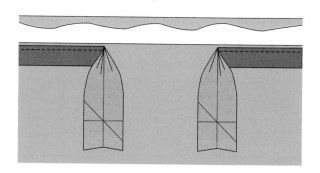

1. Matching right sides and diagonal lines, pin binding ends together at right angles (**Fig. 24**).

Fig. 24

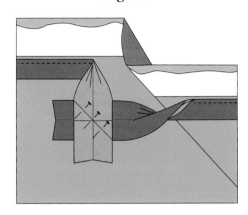

12. Machine stitch along diagonal line, removing pins as you stitch (**Fig. 25**).

Fig. 25

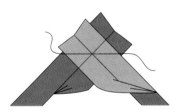

13. Lay binding against quilt to double-check that it is correct length.
14. Trim binding ends, leaving $1/4$" seam allowance; press seam open. Stitch binding to quilt.
15. Trim backing and batting a scant $1/4$" larger than quilt top so that batting and backing will fill the binding when it is folded over to quilt backing.

16. On one edge of quilt, fold binding over to quilt backing and pin pressed edge in place, covering stitching line (**Fig. 26**). On adjacent side, fold binding over, forming a mitered corner (**Fig. 27**). Repeat to pin remainder of binding in place.

Fig. 26   **Fig. 27**

17. Blindstitch binding to backing, taking care not to stitch through to front of quilt. To blindstitch, come up at 1, go down at 2, and come up at 3 (**Fig. 28**). Length of stitches may be varied as desired.

Fig. 28

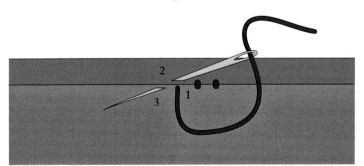

SIGNING AND DATING YOUR QUILT

A completed quilt is a work of art and should be signed and dated. There are many different ways to do this and numerous books on the subject. The label should reflect the style of the quilt, the occasion or person for which it was made, and the quilter's own particular talents. Following are suggestions for recording the history of quilt or adding a sentiment for future generations.

- Embroider quilter's name, date, and any additional information on quilt top or backing. Matching floss, such as cream floss on white background, will leave a subtle record. Bright or contrasting floss will make the information stand out.
- Make label from muslin and use permanent marker to write information. Use different colored permanent markers to make label more decorative. Stitch label to back of quilt.
- Piece an extra block from quilt top pattern to use as label. Add information with permanent fabric pen. Appliqué block to back of quilt.
- The labels provided here may be scanned or photocopied and photo transferred to white or cream fabric. Stitch label to back of quilt.

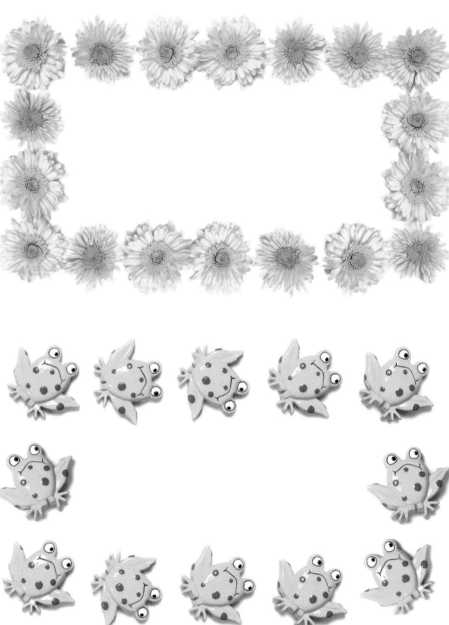

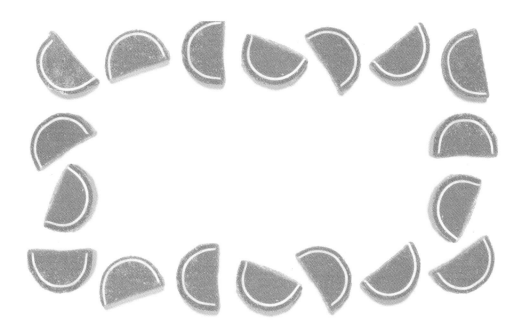

Metric Conversion Chart

Inches x 2.54 = centimeters (cm)
Inches x 25.4 = millimeters (mm)
Inches x .0254 = meters (m)

Yards x .9144 = meters (m)
Yards x 91.44 = centimeters (cm)
Centimeters x .3937 = inches (")
Meters x 1.0936 = yards (yd)

Standard Equivalents

1/8"	3.2 mm	0.32 cm	1/8 yard	11.43 cm	0.11 m
1/4"	6.35 mm	0.635 cm	1/4 yard	22.86 cm	0.23 m
3/8"	9.5 mm	0.95 cm	3/8 yard	34.29 cm	0.34 m
1/2"	12.7 mm	1.27 cm	1/2 yard	45.72 cm	0.46 m
5/8"	15.9 mm	1.59 cm	5/8 yard	57.15 cm	0.57 m
3/4"	19.1 mm	1.91 cm	3/4 yard	68.58 cm	0.69 m
7/8"	22.2 mm	2.22 cm	7/8 yard	80 cm	0.8 m
1 "	25.4 mm	2.54 cm	1 yard	91.44 cm	0.91 m

Notes

Editorial Staff

Vice President and Editor-in-Chief Sandra Graham Case
Executive Publications Director Cheryl Nodine Gunnells
Senior Publications Director Susan White Sullivan
Quilt Publications Director Cheryl Johnson
Designer Relations Director Debra Nettles
Art Operations Director Jeff Curtis
Art Publications Director Rhonda Shelby
Art Catagory Manager Lora Puls
Art Imaging Director Mark Hawkins
Technical Writer Lisa Lancaster
Editorial Writer Susan McManus Johnson
Graphic Artist Ashley Carozza
Imaging Technician Mark R. Potter
Photographer Lloyd Litsey
Photography Stylist Jan Nobles
Publishing Systems Administrator Becky Riddle
Publishing Systems Assistants Clint Hanson, Josh Hyatt, and John Rose

Business Staff

Chief Operating Officer Tom Siebenmorgen
Vice President, Sales and Marketing Pam Stebbins
Sales and Services Director Margaret Reinold
Vice President, Operations Jim Dittrich
Comptroller, Operations Rob Thieme
Retail Customer Service Manager Stan Raynor
Print Production Manager Fred F. Pruss